HOW TO BECOME A CAREER COACH

An unconventional guide to building
a thriving career coaching business
(even when you're not sure where to start)

SCOTT ANTHONY BARLOW

How to Become A Career Coach: An unconventional guide to building a thriving career coaching business (even when you're not sure where to start)

Copyright © 2015 by Scott Anthony Barlow. All rights reserved.

Unless otherwise indicated, the information and materials available in this book are the property of the author and are protected under U.S. and foreign copyright, trademark, and other intellectual property laws. You may not reproduce or distribute copies of materials found in this book in any form (including by e-mail or other electronic means) without prior written permission from the author. Requests for permission to reproduce or distribute materials found in book should be sent to Scott@happentoyourcareer.com.

Limit of Liability/Disclaimer of Warranties

The information provided and commented upon in these materials is designed to provide guidance only and are not to be used as a substitute for professional judgment. Any person consulting these materials is solely responsible for implementation of this guidance as it relates to the particular matter for which the end user refers to these materials. Implied warranties of merchantability and fitness of purpose, if any exist, and all other warranties, expressed or implied, are expressly waived by any user of these materials. The author shall not be liable for any direct, indirect, special, or consequential damages, including, without limitation, attorneys' fees or costs arising from any use of these guides or the information or material contained herein.

ISBN: 9781092671927

To Mackenzie, Camden, and Grayson

If you're willing to work for it, you can do or be almost anything!

But if instead you focus on your strengths and what you can't stop doing, you'll most certainly change the world!

To Alyssa

Thanks for enabling me to do all that I can't stop doing. And for inspiring me to write my own book! You continue to amaze me even after all these years!

Contents

The Decade Behind Overnight Success — 7
   You can avoid some mistakes (if you know which ones are most important) — 15
   Your own 'decade to overnight success' didn't just start today — 16
   Your path to success will be your own, not mine — 16

How to Get the Most Out of This Book — 23
   How long will it take to build a coaching business? — 30

Is Creating a Coaching Business That Meets My Needs Really Possible? — 39
   How do I know I actually want to become a career coach full-time? — 41

What's the Path to Becoming a Career Coach? — 47
   Path #1: Work as a coach for a trade group, jobs organization, or educational institution — 49
   Path #2: Work with an organization that provides coaching as a service — 50
   Path #3: Run your own coaching practice or business — 50

Where Should I Get Started? What Do I Need to Do? — 59
   Trying to be Everywhere — 61
   Trying to help everyone — 62
   The prettiest website wins (or does it?) — 64

How Do I Learn to Run a Business — 69
   Top-performers focus on a specific goal or need — 70
   After you have defined the goal, what is the shortest or most effective way to make it happen? — 71

How Do I Sell Coaching?	75
Where Do I Find Coaching Clients?	87
The real question is: 'What does knowing your Target Market actually do for you?'	90
How Do I Package a Coaching Offer?	101
Crash Course on Salary Negotiation	106
How to Attract People by Allowing Them to Self-select	111
How to get people to raise their hand to say they're interested in working with you	112
What is a Client Attraction Magnet?	113
What does this Client Attraction Magnet do for them?	116
What is it actually? (How does it work behind the scenes)	116
Here's some questions to ask when getting ready to create a Client Attraction Magnet	120
How to Pull Off the Not-So-Magic Trick of Generating Traffic	123
What on earth is 'traffic' really?	123
Buying traffic (paying for peeps!)	124
Building an audience	126
Borrowing traffic	128
How Put It on Autopilot	133
What you need to build an automated Client Attraction System	135
What Does a Thriving Business Look Like?	137
OPTION #1: Work with 8 clients per month	138
OPTION #2: 11 Clients	139
OPTION #3: Mixed coaching, courses and speaking business	140
How Do I Make Sure That I'm Successful As a Career Coach?	141

The Decade Behind Overnight Success

When I was finishing college in 2005, I had just received my first "professional job offer" before I even finished school.

My family and friends all made sure I knew how lucky I was to have a job offer before I finished school.

I wasn't super-excited about the job or the company, but I didn't know what else I would do if I didn't take it. So at the ripe old age of 23 years, I reasoned that everyone must be correct with this job offer, and that "I had made it."

After all, this job paid more than I thought was possible fresh out of college, I was going to be leading a team of 20 and, if I did really well the first year, they would buy me a BMW. Up until this point, I'd never even ridden in a BMW, let alone thought it would be a reality to own one.

I had also just been married to Alyssa, my high school sweetheart. We were very ready to begin our lives together, so I accepted the role and moved her to Portland, Oregon, the "City of Bridges."

At first, everything seemed pretty great. We bought a beautiful house that was twice as expensive as what my parents had ever owned at the time. We made all the trips to Home Depot and painted every wall in the place in designer colors. We ate out at expensive restaurants and, from every normal societal standard, we were doing pretty well.

Until you started looking under the surface.

The Truth is: Every single day I was commuting three grueling hours a day on Interstate 5 to a job where I was spending 70-80-hour weeks, including weekends, never seeing Alyssa and instead spending almost 100% of my time stressed out.

It was affecting my health. I gained almost 50 pounds growing to a pudgy 230+ pounds for the first time in my life. I started noticing that I was winded going up a set of stairs. I started having panic attacks in the morning traffic on the way into work. Actually, I didn't know they were panic attacks until later on. I just knew I was having trouble breathing and in tears and freaking out in my car. Someone probably could have told me that these lovely little episodes were called panic attacks, but

I didn't tell anyone. I was embarrassed that I "couldn't hack it in the real world."

This was made worse because, instead of concentrating on my work, I couldn't get my ADD brain to focus on what I was supposed to be doing at any given time. Instead I found myself sitting at my desk inventing ways out.

What if I jumped out the second story window of my office? I reasoned that the fall would probably just break a leg or two. I thought about this very deliberately wondering if workers comp insurance would cover my fall so I could have two weeks off without being stressed out?

In fact, it got so bad I remember one day when I went to the burger joint right next door to my office in the Rose Quarter of Portland and ordered three hamburgers, a large fries and a ginormous huckleberry milkshake. I was hopeful that I would make myself sick enough to have an excuse to go home that day and hide from work.

Unfortunately, it didn't work and I just spent the rest of the day in pain, huddled over my laptop pretending to answer email.

Obviously it was a bad situation. Actually "bad situation" probably doesn't even begin to cover the life-shortening, food-medicated, lonely, stress-induced panic that was my first year of "big kid work" in the "real world."

One day on my 3-hour commute, traffic was inexplicably stopped yet again. I remember looking around at stopped traffic at all the somber faces in the other cars, wondering if this was what it was like for everyone. As I looked into the windshields and door windows of Subarus and Mercedes, nobody looked really happy. I remember feeling even more hopeless.

This couldn't be how work life was. This was terrible!

After about a year of this, I decided I couldn't take it any longer. I had to do something. There was no way I could go through another 40 years of this drudgery. Plus, at the rate I was going, I figured I wouldn't make it 40 more years with all the stress-induced huckleberry milkshakes and multiple cheeseburgers per sitting.

I finally got the courage to go to my boss and talk to him about it. I called him up and I was super nervous to have the discussion. I told him I didn't feel like this job was a great fit. Then I braced for whatever came next.

He listened, and he asked me a few questions. Actually it felt good. I was so relieved to finally have it out on the table. He even said he felt the exact same way. And clearly, he did... because three weeks later he called all of the people that I worked with into the office under the pretext of a "training" and let me know that he was firing me. I could either accept three months' severance and go tell all of my former coworkers who had been gathered waiting for the "training" to begin that I was leaving the company, OR I could take two weeks pay and walk out then and there.

Yeah, I know! it wasn't the ending that I expected either.

It was like I was on some kind of crazy game show.

> *[ANNOUNCER VOICE] You've already (pre-emptively) won fast-food-caused heart disease for a future undetermined date. We're also going to give you morning commute-induced panic attacks. But that's not all! You have a choice to make! You can choose Door #1 where we pay you 10 weeks of salary to swallow your pride and choose utter embarrassment in front of all your colleagues and former direct reports, or Door #2 where you admit defeat and accept total failure and shame by not providing for your family.*

After trying unsuccessfully not to shed 24-year-old guy tears, I wiped my face and chose door number 1.

I don't actually remember what was said or what I said during my stint at the front of the room with nearly 20 of the people who I'd worked closely with for over a year, but I'm sure my face was the color of maraschino cherries that they put on top of all the banana splits that had helped me through the previous 12 months.

My next memory was getting in my car for my slow commute home in the rain. I spent almost 45 minutes procrastinating about picking up my cellphone to call Alyssa and tell her "yes I brought you to Portland away from all of your family and I have no job or anything to show for it."

This was horrible and I wouldn't wish this set of events on anyone, but I'm not sharing all of this with you because I want you to feel sorry for me. Actually, exactly the opposite. This became one of the best gifts I could ever have received at 24 years old.

In that moment, driving home in the rain, after hanging up the phone with Alyssa, I made myself a promise. I decided that I would never live like this again. Ever! I knew that I had to figure out how to do work that didn't stress me out to the max. There had to be something out there that didn't make me feel this way. Maybe even something that I actually enjoyed?

This single decision sent me on a decade-long journey to learn how to live without settling in my career (and all aspects of life). I wanted to learn how to live what was most important to me; I didn't want to be thrown around by life and my work circumstances. I wanted to understand how and why a few people are able to grab the reins and live out life in the way they want to and why others feel like they are forever at the mercy of whatever is thrown their way.

But back then, driving home in the rain, just after getting off my cellphone and telling her the bad news, I had no idea that this one single decision to no longer settle would later lead me to getting many of my dream jobs, and career changing into many fields including human resources, operations, training, talent acquisition, and marketing across many industries.

It led me to interview over 100 times in seven years for career opportunities I badly wanted. It led me to find a way to move into human resources leadership with no experience. That led to being on the other side of the desk and interviewing 2,000 other people. I got to learn to become a master coach and to coach leaders and executives (all funded by the companies I worked for). It caused me to learn how to influence my bosses to change my roles to fit what I wanted to focus my time and effort on.

That single decision at 24 acted as the catalyst to learn what I really wanted out of work and then find those opportunities in the unlikeliest of places — opportunities that I enjoyed immensely and where my employers happily paid me whatever I requested.

Most of all, a decade later when I decided that I wanted to run my own business, I realized that people were already coming to me for advice. I was already having "coaching conversations" with coworkers, friends, and acquaintances about their careers.

Plus, I was enjoying it. I found I was excited to help people avoid the despair that plagued my first job. I enjoyed helping them focus on what gave them purpose and fulfillment without giving up the pay and lifestyle they wanted.

I decided that I had to build a business doing exactly that. Over the next three 3 years, I became committed to making the move to coaching full-time.

It was the most difficult thing that I've ever done. I learned to get up at 3:55 a.m. every day, and I worked many Saturdays watching my kids play in the yard. I learned copy-writing, digital marketing, messaging, how to put together digital training programs, conducting webinars, podcasts, and how to serve coaching clients at a higher level than I thought possible.

I know that everything else out there is going to make running a coaching business sound super sexy and will give you a "Photoshopped" version of what running a thriving coaching business looks like.

It would be super easy for me to do that. There are lots of benefits and upsides and it's allowed me and my family to live a completely different type of life than I ever could have otherwise.

That said, I want you to know that behind every single successful business is some kind of hardship, overcoming difficulty, or sacrifice of some sort.

I think Winston Churchill had it right when he said:

> *"Success is stumbling from failure to failure with no loss of enthusiasm."*
> **Winston Churchill**

I'm telling you this for 3 reasons:

1. You can avoid some mistakes (if you know which ones are most important)

I've learned that many of the mistakes I made in building a business can be entirely avoided and that's why I have helped career coaches get their start the last five years. It's also why I created the Professional Career Coach Training and Certification program and it's why I wrote this book for you. If it's important for you to build a career coaching practice, I want to help you make this transition faster so you can focus on making a life for yourself.

2. Your own 'decade to overnight success' didn't just start today

The second reason is that I want you to realize that behind every single success story is often many years of hard work, experience, blood, sweat, tears and sometimes too many huckleberry milkshakes.

No matter how much time and effort I help you save, if you want to become a career coach and build a thriving career-coaching business, it's not going to be easy! If it was, then everyone would do it.

The great thing here is that you've already had many experiences and challenges in your life up until now that are already contributing to your own "decade to overnight success." You don't start fresh when you make the decision to become a career coach.

Instead, look for opportunities to leverage your current experiences, strengths, and even your past story. This, combined with this guide, is what will help you to actually move at a faster rate.

3. Your path to success will be your own, not mine

The last reason I'm telling you this is because the most common question I get is "how did you start this business?" Then people find out I got up at 3:55 am every day and are thinking: *I don't even like getting up before 6 a.m. Do I have to get up early, if so is 4:15 a.m. good enough?*

I wrote this book in the form of a guide not because it will lay out a perfect path for you. Instead, it will help you find your own way and your own path. You don't have to do exactly what I did. In fact, now that I've been through it myself and helped hundreds of other people start successful businesses, I wouldn't recommend some of what I did. In many cases, I've since learned that there are better ways.

The better ways don't incorporate going and getting all of the same experience that I had when I started. Instead, they take into account the experiences you have along with the type of coaching business that you want to create. They take into account your strengths.

So no, you don't have to wake up at the crack of dawn, unless you're determined to; no, you don't have to go get HR experience, unless you love HR; no, you don't have to interview 2,000 people and hear their crazy stories as they pine for jobs they are way overqualified for (unless you can't get enough of the crazy stories that people tell, which I can't).

You do have to be willing to accept that you have your own experiences and that they are valuable. You have to be open to accepting that you will make mistakes and that's just part of the process. Most of all, you have to be open to allowing your strengths, which will be different than mine, to shine through so that clients can't wait to work with you.

There isn't one strengths and talents set that makes up a great coach. We've seen this with measuring the assessment results of those people who we've worked with over the years that are or have become coaches. Even when you ask full time coaches that have been doing this a long time what makes a great coach the answer is often mixed and there isn't one set of tangible experiences talents or skills.

In fact here's some examples of responses from full time coaches that are at the top of their game.

> *To be an exceptional career coach you need to have a structured methodology to help make everything from the self assessment to landing a job less abstract and digestible, you must be consultative in your contracting approach with your clients to understand their challenges, goals, timelines, fears, and learning styles, and you need to be willing to roll up your sleeves and get your hands dirty when it comes to getting your clients personal branding docs created/updated. Probably the most important thing that we forget as career coaches: practice what you preach so your clients get inspired not just by your words, but rather by your actions.*
>
> **— Eli Bohemond**

...someone to guide them with effective strategies because what they were doing was not working. Easy to talk to -- they said they felt really comfortable opening up and never felt like they were being judged, rather they were being championed and challenged in a supportive way.

— Emily Liou, PHR, ELI-MP

1. Qualities: I love coaches who are authentic, confident yet humble, and positive. 2. Skills: They are great at providing a perspective shift that gets their client unstuck. 3. Strategy: A great career coach provides an effective strategy or framework to help their clients reach their goals.

— Mo Chanmugham

an amazing Career Coach needs to have the courage to tell their clients what they need to hear, not just what they want to hear. It's striking a balance between being supportive and shifting old habits that have been keeping them stuck, often for years.

— Cindy Harvey

1/ trusting relationship with client that allows for vulnerability 2/ ability to see and directly tackle root cause 3/ Demonstrate and teach positive mindset

— Avery Roth

The differences in every one of these responses are vast but there are a few commonalities that most coaches (and their clients) agree upon that make the best coaches.

- You can build a trusting relationship with your clients that allows them to be vulnerable with you.
- You are willing to tell your clients what no one else in their life is willing to.
- You have an effective strategy or framework that helps clients get results.

There is nothing in here about having a Doctorate in Psychology or being amazing at chess or even that you have to have certain strengths or experience or credentials.

The first two (building trusting relationships and telling your clients what noone else will) are skillsets that require practice but nearly anyone can become great at. The third (effective strategy or framework) is something that can be obtained through a highly effective coaching training program.

Full transparency: I own a company that offers career coaching specific training and certification however as you'll see in our later chapter titled "What's the Path to Become a Career Coach?" that this is only one of a variety of ways to learn a structured framework and build your coaching skills.

That said, the big secret to how we help others become successful coaches is not duplicating everything I've done or other coaches have done. It's using your own strengths and experiences to help select a path that works for you so you have help your clients get results and so you can .

This simple strategy of building on what you already have instead of thinking you have to do it the way I did, is what actually cuts away years of pain and mistakes.

It's what will allow you to build the business of your dreams, give you very large amounts of flexibility, allow you to work where ever you want, and create a coaching business foundation that removes limits from your income.

All of that said, this guide will help make it possible for you to think differently about building a thriving coaching business, provided you know how to use it. That's exactly what we'll cover in the next chapter!

How to Get the Most Out of This Book

When I was still working a full-time corporate job in Human Resources leadership and had been running Happen to Your Career for a couple years part-time on the side, it was just starting to work really well. I was reaching people I'd never met in other parts of the world and then they were emailing me asking to talk about coaching.

Back in those days, I always looked at my business email in the early morning, because 3:55 a.m. comes early and I learned that it would jar me awake and often get my brain excited and thinking about the possibilities of the day.

One morning, I woke up to a particularly interesting email. A reader of my *Happen To Your Career* website and podcast listener had sent me a note asking, "do you offer any type of training or certification to teach others to become career coaches?" She went on to say that she didn't want to reinvent the wheel and instead wanted to learn from someone who was already having success.

I was flattered but at that time I didn't yet feel like I was having success.

Even though I was regularly bringing in thousands of dollars a month in revenue — much more than the average "part-time" coaching business — I still hadn't replaced my six-figure income from my day job and gone full-time.

In my head, this felt like I "wasn't yet qualified to do something like this."

But over the following years as I transitioned to running a full-time coaching business and then hiring and training career coaches to bring onto our team, I kept getting the same type of request over and over again.

At first, I started working with those who were willing to pay for my coaching fees, and I started working with them one-on-one. Then I began taking on fewer coaching clients of any kind and instead focusing more on supporting my team. The requests kept coming and I had two major realizations.

- There wasn't a clear path for career coaches and so many talented potential coaches might never start working with clients if I didn't do something to make it easier to start.

- We were having ridiculous success results that other career coaches weren't having. I knew that I couldn't help everyone in the world that needed career help. I also knew not everyone would resonate with my brand. In my mind, this meant that I had to start doing something to train the next set of up-and-coming career coaches. So I started researching the market and talking to existing career coaches and people who wanted to become career coaches to learn what they wanted and needed (and what they think they want and need, but we know they don't).

That was several years before I started writing this book. Now my team and I talk to career coaches and those who want to become career coaches every single day. Since 2013, I've personally interacted with more than 500 career coaches (which I highly suspect makes me the person in the world who's talked to more career coaches than anyone else. I really have no way to validate this though).

Since my team and I talk to current and aspiring career coaches constantly, we get a lot of questions about how to become a career coach and how to start a successful business when coaching. It's my goal to answer as many of those questions in this book as I possibly can.

In fact, you'll find that the chapters are structured around answering those questions for you.

You'll also find that this isn't structured in the exact same way as a normal book or guide.

First of all, it's shorter than your average book. So short that the full title barely squeezes onto the spine of the book.

This length (or lack of length) is intentional, because we've learned that new career coaches are addicted to information, partially because most of us are learners and never want to stop learning. We enjoy the process of learning too much!

When we talk to new or aspiring coaches, they say things like, "I'm trying to soak up everything I can."

This sounds great in theory. It's also the type of advice that you hear from "newbies" in all areas and realms of life. For example, my son just recently got that advice when he started playing hockey and most of the other kids had been playing for several years already.

We find that, while it's "good advice," it's actually incomplete.

Soak up everything you can from where? How? In what area? What do I do about the contradictory soakings that I get, but really don't fully understand? How long do I soak?

Is this bathtub-and-bath salts-with-candles level soaking? Or a water-balloon-fight-on-a-hot-day type of soaking?

We've seen that, for most new coaches or coaches growing a business, that "Good Advice" can be detrimental.

You end up in what I call "Educated Overwhelm."

This is where you've learned a lot, but still don't have the answers for yourself.

It's detrimental and defeating because, even though you know that you should do something about picking a market and building your website, and getting and email list set up, you still have no idea what you should begin with, what is really most important, and how to move forward.

It leaves you feeling like you're still just as far away from building a thriving coaching business as you were when you started learning. It also makes you feel like you've wasted a bunch of time (and in many cases you have).

It's also why I didn't write a 400-page book showing you in detail how to build a $400,000 coaching business, complete with "sales funnels," and Google keyword domination in all the categories that you want to be known for owning.

You have to create your first clients before you can build the $5,000-a-month business. And you have to build the $5,000-a-month business before you can build the six-figure business, and so on.

My experience is that many of us want to jump right to knowing how the big coaching business works. My experience also shows me that that's not very useful information for you because you can dream all you want about the $5 million business you want to build, but if you don't actually help your first 5, 10, 25, 100 clients, then you don't get to cross that golden bridge of possibility. Instead, what's much more useful is to get you to the point where you have not only your first clients, but then understand what the next steps are to build that into a full-time business.

That is exactly what this unconventional guide will do.

- It will help you understand where to focus your time and effort in the beginning stages of your business (and help you understand where you don't have to spend your time and effort as well so you can avoid educated overwhelm.).

- It will help you answer the most common questions that hundreds of aspiring career coaches have asked. When you're starting out, you don't even really know what to ask. You might think you're asking about the most important things, but once you have the experience of having turned into a professional coach, you realize that many of them aren't useful questions.

- I'm going answer those questions, but along the way I'm going to help you ask the questions you wouldn't even know to ask and teach you to ask better questions, which as a coach, will help you ask better questions of your future clients and get them better results.

- It will provide you the most important actions you can take (if your goal is to build a full-time or part-time coaching business). This will save you time and frustration, and when you apply the learning, it will help you avoid years of making the same exact mistakes that every other coach makes.

Also here's what this guide won't do.

- It won't teach you to coach — that's something that is best done through practice and application. (We do teach coaching, in our Professional Career Coach Training and Certification program; you can learn more about that at: https://becomeacareercoach.com/certification

- It won't provide you every single step to make everything work perfectly. I will show you examples and specifics, but when you are the CEO of your own coaching business, you are accepting the responsibility of figuring out how to integrate the teachings and frameworks into the business you want to create. If you don't want that responsibility, don't start a business where you're the sole employee.

How long will it take to build a coaching business?

Imagine that you're in a new city you've never been to before. You and your partner decide that you want to find a nice restaurant and try out a new dining experience.

You get out your mobile phone and with your travel app you find one that's highly recommended. You're excited! The menu looks great. The pictures on TripAdvisor are already causing you to salivate! The dessert menu with its array of delightfully covered chocolate... Ok ok, let's just say you're excited.

You call up the restaurant. The maitre d' answers the phone and asks how they can help.

You tell them that you found them on Google and that they come pretty highly recommended and then you ask, "How long will it take?"

The helpful maitre d' on the other end is puzzled, "How long will what take?"

That's when you drop the bomb on them.

"How long will it take for me to come in and eat my meal and finish and pay and leave."

Ok I know you wouldn't do that; it doesn't make sense. There are so many variables that the maitre d' doesn't know at all.

They don't know how big your party is. They don't know when you want to arrive; they don't even yet know if they can seat you!

Plus, even if they did know all of that information, they have no way of knowing whether you're the type of customer who will take four hours to enjoy their meal or if you'll scarf down half of it in 15 minutes and get the rest to go.

That's not to mention that, if you just order appetizers and that's all that you want, you'll probably have all your food sooner than if you're planning on a five-course meal (after all, they have chocolate on the dessert menu!)

You simply wouldn't ask something like that.

So why when it comes to a career-coaching business is one of the most common questions we get: "how long does it take?"

As you might suspect, even if I know a huge amount about you, the answer is going to vary widely depending on your goals, how much time you devote to the business, your existing skill sets, what type of business you want to build, who you want to serve with your business, and many, many other variables.

I personally wanted to build a business that was generating six figures in revenue before leaving my full-time job as an HR leader. I wanted to serve top-performing professionals who had already had a track record of success in their career. I wanted to build a team around the business and not just myself when I stepped into it. I also was interested in building a coaching program that didn't exist and could be the best in the world for the type of people I was looking to help. This wasn't my first business, I had hardly any digital marketing experience, but I taught sales. It took me almost exactly three years from when I started the business to build to that level of income and step into it full-time.

I tell you that about myself, but your variables and timelines will be different. We've helped more than enough people make this type of transition to know that yours might be shorter and it might be longer.

Asking "How Long Will It Take?" isn't a very useful question for you.

I want to be really clear with you in this book: Most people in the world will never take the steps to build a full-time (or even part-time) business. It's not because they can't and it's not because they aren't capable of it. Instead, it's primarily because they can't see all of the steps and don't have a guarantee about how long it's going to take.

As human beings, we are hard-wired to steer clear of uncertainty (some of us more than others). This means that the single-biggest killer of businesses before they ever start is the lack of a truthful clear answer to: "how long will this take?"

Most people will be unwilling to put in the effort without knowing that it will lead to a certain outcome.

I'm perfectly fine with that fact. It spells opportunity for those of us who are willing to commit to figuring out opportunities that have a lot of variables.

In a moment I'll share with you the single-biggest difference I see with those coaches who turn career coaching into a thriving full-time business versus those who close up shop and blame it on the economy or worse... that they had another opportunity that "they couldn't turn down" (which sometimes is true, but usually is code for "I couldn't make it work").

First, though, I will indulge you with some indirect answers to the "How long does it take?" question, with the caveat that nobody, not me or you, can predict how long it will take.

Looking back on the folks who I've witnessed build a successful business, it takes them between 18 months and six years.

I'm very aware that this is a very broad range, but you have to remember every single one of those people had different goals (some are just trying make $2,000 a month regularly; others need to replace a $175K salary).

I've only coached a few people who said "wow, that was way less time than I thought." Those were people who came in with very low expectations like "I just want to prove to myself that I can make $3,000 in coaching revenue."

Most people fall into the other category. This sounds something like: "I want to go full-time in two years."

The question I always ask them is, if it took you three years instead of two to generate a full-time income, would that still be good for you? Most of the time they say, "Yes, absolutely." Some of the time they say, "No," and then when I begin digging, we realize together that maybe they are interested in building a coaching business for the wrong reasons.

Here's why I ask that type of question:

The people who I always see move the fastest and reach their goals the quickest are those who come in with a completely different mentality.

It's those who come in with the "no matter what" mentality.

It's actually one of the things we look for when we're deciding who makes it into our Professional Career Coach Certification program.

Here's how it shows up.

I spoke with a candidate yesterday who had applied for our Professional Career Coaching Training program and had already had a conversation with our team.

When I asked her what her goals were, she said "I already know this is right for me, so I need to figure this out no matter what. However, I really want to make this into my full-time income in less than five years. Preferably sooner."

She went on to say that's why she'd applied for the program; she knew that one of the ways she could reach her goal sooner was by learning from other people who have done this already.

Now contrast that with the other, less-successful, mentality. Those people say things like, "Well do you think it will take more than 12 months? Because I'm not sure if I want to go down this path if I can't guarantee that I'll produce a good income in that time."

Here's the irony: those who come in with the "no matter what" mentality are much more likely to have it take a shorter amount of time than those who are placing high artificial constraints on themselves that nobody can accurately predict.

This means that a much more useful question to ask, rather than "how long will this take?" is: "Do I believe that building a career coaching business is right for me."

I'm guessing you wouldn't be reading this book if you didn't already have a high degree of interest in running a coaching business. If you already know the answer is "Heck Yeah!" Awesome you can skip the questions I'm going to suggest, but if you're undecided, here are some questions that we use behind the scenes to coach people on the fence about whether building a business is right for you.

- If you were at the end of your life and hadn't ever started a coaching business, would you regret it?

- Do you really love coaching or just love the idea of it?

- What are the biggest reasons that you want to build a coaching business? Are those achievable in other ways? If you can satisfy those in other ways do you think a coaching business would still be your first choice?

- Do you enjoy doing lots of things or would you prefer to spend most of your time coaching? (In a coaching business it's not uncommon to spend 15-40% of your time coaching and the rest of it operating or building the business)

If you believe a coaching business is right for you, then ask yourself another question: "If it takes longer than I think, will that still be a great situation for me?"

I use this technique all the time. If becoming a millionaire takes you 12 years instead of 10, do you still believe it will be worth it?

If it took you 10 months to become certified instead of 6, would that still be a good thing for you?

Or a personal example from my past: It took me a year longer than I wanted before I was able to leave my full time job in HR leadership than I thought it might (I wanted to replace my full time income in 2 years. it took me 3). I also took me a year longer than I expected before I was able to hire my first full-time team member at Happen To Your Career.

Was it worth the journey even though it took longer than I expected?

Heck Yeah! You better believe it! I suspect that if you're really determined to build a career-coaching business even if it takes a little longer than you think it might, it would still be worth it for you!

The question everyone asks:

How long does it take?

A far better (and more useful set of questions):

Is building a coaching business really what I want? if it takes longer than I think, will that still be a better situation for me than never having done it?

Remember the people who are most successful at building a coaching business are those who say, "I'm going to figure out how to make this work for me, no matter how long it takes"

Is Creating a Coaching Business That Meets My Needs Really Possible?

A LOT OF US have this dream of being able to work where and how we want to.

We imagine ourselves being able to travel and still get work done. Or going to visit friends or relatives any time we want because, guess what?!!, we don't have to be in a particular office at a particular time.

I've done all of this. It's not for everyone, but I personally think it's awesome and life-changing.

Imagine being able to go to Italy for a month and not miss a beat with your work and income. You could take in the Roman architecture and art during the day and spend a couple hours during the evening coaching your clients and helping change their lives and careers. After you wrap up your client conversations, you relax on the veranda with a glass of 4-year-old Chianti (which you know from your conversation earlier in the day about wines with the Italian shop owner that Chianti is best at 4-7 years old).

I spent four weeks in Paris in 2017 with my wife and three kids, working from coworking spaces and my AirBnB while experiencing what it was actually like to live and work there. Then four weeks in 2018 in the UK with my family only working about eight hours a week.

It turns out travel isn't the only reason I love having an incredibly flexible schedule.

As I was writing this, my son got sick with the flu, so I canceled one of my appointments and picked him up from school and we went home and huddled up in blankets and watched a Spiderman movie.

That type of flexibility and autonomy is amazing. It changes what your life feels like. Imagine for a second what would change for you if you had that kind of flexibility and control over your schedule.

I've been studying career and human happiness for well over 10 years and have seen in the research how much of a difference this makes. In our business, where we work with clients, we witness that, when you consistently feel like you have direct influence in "how the work gets done" (autonomy) and "when/where it gets done" (flexibility), you see an increase in feelings of happiness.

This appears to be backed up in the data and research we've curated over the years. For a complete look at career happiness collection of research, studies, books and more, you can visit https://becomeacareercoach.com/bonus.

Here's what I've also learned over the years: The need and desire for that type of autonomy and flexibility alone is not reason enough to become a career coach (or coach of any kind for that matter).

Why?

Because the work to get you there is hard. It may become one of the most difficult things that you have done. So we see that those who have a greater purpose and reason for taking the path of becoming a career coach are much more likely to be successful.

Translation: Just serving yourself isn't enough for you to become a successful career coach and run a thriving business.

How do I know I actually want to become a career coach full-time?

If you're reading this right now, you're either interested in building and growing a coaching business OR you're trying to decide if becoming a career coach is right for you.

In either of those cases, I'm guessing that there are a few things that you want out of the deal.

I'm guessing you want to help others and pursue a career that you find fulfilling.

I'm also guessing that you enjoy making a big impact in someone's life in a very positive way.

For me personally, the first time I thought about it, I knew that I wanted to be around for my kids and that I wanted to help people completely change and improve their lives.

However, most of those exact same people don't see how they can make a living at it or how to make it possible for themselves.

This might be you too.

But how do you know if it's where you should double-down your efforts?

That might be you if you're the type of person who for some crazy reason people just keep coming to for advice, OR you're that person who people want to share everything with.

Maybe you know that, even though you can be a high-performer working for someone else, you really want to actually be working for yourself.

You probably enjoy helping other people and probably also appreciate how some businesses can do a lot of good for people and the world.

Depending on how far along on this journey you are, you might have already had a few clients you've helped out.

You might even have a website where you're just not sure how to use it to attract clients or truly convey your expertise and establish yourself as an "authority."

You've probably had passing thoughts about a coaching certification, but wondered whether or not it would actually help get you credibility or give you what you need to make this into "a thing."

Above all, if you find that you just **can't stop** helping other people in the areas you enjoy and have learned about or have some experience in, then it's probably a great sign that you should be coaching in one form or another.

If all of the above are true, OR even just one, it's probably a safe bet that you would enjoy coaching full-time tremendously.

The real question is do you want to run a career coaching business OR just become a career coach full-time.

Running the business requires building more skill sets than just becoming a great coach.

Sales, marketing, finances are just a few of these areas that are required to own and run your own coaching business.

What I've found as I've been helping coaches over the last five years is that the real trick is to build your business so that it works with you and your clients rather than against you.

Here's an example:

Rather than doing separate "sales calls" and learning everything about "sales closes," building rapport, and finding needs, you could simply show up and coach them.

The same types of impactful coaching questions that you would ask someone in order to help them are also going to be what causes them to want to work with you.

This means that I can focus on getting really good at coaching and helping instead of separately focusing on learning to sell.

Another example was a coach I worked with who was struggling to write blog posts, but really wanted to expand the people who were finding her website.

To be clear, you can build an entire coaching business completely without a website. I've helped people do exactly this. But her goal was to be able to continually reach new people to have coaching conversations with, and she wanted to put part of that on autopilot. So she found herself writing blog posts hating every minute of it.

She thought she had to do this and that it would be the way to bring people to her website. On the other hand, she was an exceptional verbal communicator and could articulate her thoughts easily and rattle off helpful anecdotes at the drop of a hat. She also seemed to enjoy this type of communication.

I suggested to her that she stop trying to force it and instead focus on those methods and approaches that came more naturally to her.

Because she clearly was a great verbal communicator, we build out a plan for her to make podcast appearances as a guest on podcasts and to stop trying to write all of the frustrating blog posts.

Building a business is hard enough; stop going against the grain. Instead work with it (i.e. your existing strengths and experiences).

The question people always ask:

How do I know if I want to become a career coach full-time?

A far better question:

Is this something that I will regret later on if I don't give it a chance?

If the answer is yes, then continue reading and start taking the actions in this book, if the answer is "no" you might as well stop reading this book now.

What's the Path to Becoming a Career Coach?

Just in the last month alone, my team has had countless conversations with our readers and listeners asking the same types of questions about becoming a career coach or building a career-coaching business.

Nearly every one of those conversations gets around to a question that begins with, "What's the pathway to..."

...becoming a career coach?

...starting a coaching business?

...running a coaching and a speaking business?

...getting credibility as a career coach?

To be very clear, this isn't like some professions where there is a very linear pathway to make it happen. For example, if I wanted to become a lawyer in the US, then this would be the path. (image of chart below)

Of course, this is an overly simplified version and there are bar exams that need to be passed, plus you still have to get a job as a lawyer, but for the most part this is what the path looks like.

It varies much more widely when you want to become a career coach.

This is partially because the same regulations aren't in place for this profession (thank goodness!) and partially because there are simply a lot more ways to become a successful career coach. Career coaches don't have law school to force them into mastery and, quite frankly, many of the certifications out there in the world don't help you achieve this either.

This, of course, means that if you want to be a career coach you must take it upon yourself to master the craft.

My goal is to help you understand the most effective ways that you can make it a reality for yourself and to expose you to a variety of options.

I'm going to do this by organizing these paths by the end result.

Path #1: Work as a coach for a trade group, jobs organization, or educational institution

Colleges and universities around the world need to help their students get jobs after they've educated them in their respective degree or certificate programs. This is where career coaches often come in.

Some universities go the extra mile and have career coaches who also help students with large existential questions like, "what degree should I pursue," or "what career path should I go down." But at the time of this writing, those positions are mostly filled by non-coaches.

There is a trend where some organizations have begun hiring career professionals to help with development and retention of their employees, but this is still a tiny minority and many of those positions are contracted.

Two other common places that hire career coaches in this way are:

- Organizations that teach skills or trades. Example: Coding bootcamps.
- Government-related organizations that help coach people back to work. (NOTE: These are often job coach positions instead of career coach, but it varies widely.

Path #2: Work with an organization that provides coaching as a service

This would mean that you work with an organization that provides some type of career coaching for their customers or clients. The company I own is an example of an organization like that. We have coaches that have been certified through our Professional Career Coach Certification on our team.

For some of these organizations, you might function as a full- or part-time employee, but for most of them, you would work as a contractor. If you are contracting with that organization, you are often paid one of several ways:

- by the hour
- by the coaching session
- by the number of clients you support

Path #3: Run your own coaching practice or business

This one sounds obvious... or does it?

Think about this as the "Career Coach Plus" position. You're a career coach + marketer + sales + finance + whatever else the business needs (especially if you are the only person in the business).

This one pays incredibly well — or not so well — depending on how you've built the business and grow the business.

This means that your pay is not just dependent on your craft; it is also based on your skill level at building a business. You can be the best career coach in the world and not run a profitable business.

Here's one way to think about some of the differences between each of these.

	Educational Organization	Coaching Organization	Business Owner
Pay Range	$30,795 - $91,943 *Total Pay According to PayScale.com on March 26, 2019	$30/hour - $300/hour	$0 - No Limit on earnings
Do you need a degree?	Yes. Bachelor's (Typically, but not always). Some universities will give preference to advanced degrees.	Depends on the organization	Nope
Do you need a certification?	Most organizations give preference to those with certification during the application process.	Some organizations require this.	No (Certification can help with credibility in some markets, but there is no requirement except in some non-USA countries).

Ok, up until now, everything I've just shared with you seems fairly normal.

Here's where the train starts to leave the very linear tracks and takes a left turn off into a field of possibility.

When some career coaches start out, they may be interested in only pursuing one of these paths, but that seems to change once they get into it.

I've had conversations with well over 500 career coaches in the last seven years and roughly half of them pursued several of these tracks at once.

Here are a couple examples:

Mo Chanmugham works on our team at Happen To Your Career. He is a talented career coach who has made many career transitions himself, going from marketing to attorney to recruiting to career coach. He's walked the walk of career change.

He also has taken all three of these pathways. He began coaching people for free to practice and then eventually started getting a few clients of his own in his side business. From there, he became a career coach at a university and then began working with coaching organizations. Now he has his own business AND works as a coach at Happen To Your Career.

Here's what his trajectory looked like.

***

Mimi became a career coach after we started working with her. She began taking a few clients of her own and then started working with an organization called the Flatiron School as a career coach for $50/hour. Now she runs multiple businesses herself and they have evolved completely out of coaching.

***

Olivia Gamber didn't have a background in coaching, but started developing a digital course to help others with their career on the side of her job working in HR. I met her and started working with her after that and she got the first coaching clients for her business. From there, she pivoted and partnered up with a friend to create a much larger separate coaching business.

All of these examples are drastically different in the coaching experience and credentials they began with. All took completely different paths. All varied pretty drastically in the "outcomes" they wanted and several of them had multiple outcomes involved in their path.

The commonality here is the same commonality I see with successful coaches and successful businesses.

In a word: Evolution.

Each of these people; Mo, Mimi, and Olivia, continued to evolve and not stay the same.

That's how this profession is different in reality versus how people think it's going to be.

Successful career coaches don't stop learning or evolving the ways that they are helping others. Sometimes that means the organization you're working with changes. Sometimes it means the business you own is growing and evolving.

So there isn't one pathway that's right for everyone. In fact, you don't even have to only choose one pathway if you don't want to.

This can be a little scary; I personally think this can be liberating, because you could, like Mo, do all three of these at the same time.

This might mean you could lessen financial risk by working for a coaching organization part-time while building up your business. Or build your business on the side of your day job, or work for an educational institution while working with a few clients of your own.

By the way, that's part of the reason we created the Professional Career Coach Training and Certification program,[1] to make all of these pathways much easier and more streamlined for anyone who wants to become a successful career coach. It's the only program out there that fully prepares you for any combination of these pathways.

Plus, I've found that once you've done coaching and learned how to build and scale a business, it sets you up for so many ways to pivot from there.

I think of it as the best win-win-win way that I know of to start other businesses, because it's essentially "paid research" where you are legitimately helping someone solve their problem while they're ecstatic to pay you, AND you get to learn all about exactly what they need most from you to help them. Plus, when you do a really good job, they are only all too happy to recommend you to others (think testimonials! Yea!).

---

1   https://www.happentoyourcareer.com/professional-career-coach-certification/

Here's an example of just a few spinoff businesses from people who I've helped get started with coaching:

- Paid speaking (once you've built authority on a topic area, people want to know more)
- Creation of training classes and group coaching programs
- Live events and experiential events
- Online education and courses
- Consulting for corporations (for expertise in their market)
- Licensing for corporations or individuals
- Published books and other published works

The possibilities are truly endless.

Coaching is far and away one of the best business models that allow you to easily pivot to other revenue streams inside your business and evolve to a completely different business model relatively easily.

Additionally as we'll see in our later chapter on "Traffic" each of these areas listed above can actually help you create additional 1 on 1 clients in your business as well. This means lots of possibilities for you as you evolve your coaching business and how you want to help people in the future.

So where do we get started then?

Where to start, as it turns out, is the subject of our next chapter!

> **The question people always ask:**
>
> *What's the path to become a career coach?*
>
> **A far better question:**
>
> *What's the best path for me based on my goals?*
>
> Remember there is not a perfect path to become a career coach. Also, what's right for one person, isn't right for the next person. Evaluate what you really want and then begin asking those who have more experience.

Where Should I Get Started? What Do I Need to Do?

Let me first get something out ***rant ensuing ... now*** There are a billion (ok, not a billion, but a lot) people who call themselves coaches out there.

At one point, I hesitated to even call myself a coach because it's so low of a barrier to entry. Pretty much anyone can hang out a shingle and many people have unintentionally made a mockery out of the title because it's become so well-used.

Here's the sad state of truth right now.

When you see the title "coach" after someone's name, it's a pretty safe bet to assume that:

- It's not the main source of income for that person (read: it's their side hobby).

- That person is broke because they struggle to get clients and spend most of their day perusing Facebook and leaving comments in various groups *hoping* they will hook some clients.
- That person is paid by an organization and NOT running it as their own business.

I'm over that now ***END RANT*** and I prefer to dedicate a portion of my time to making sure that the people I work with are elevating coaching as a profession and a business. We've actually even gone so far as to create a Career Coaching Certification[2] and training to help elevate the profession. I even created a podcast called "How to Become a Career Coach" to showcase the stories and pathways of successful coaches (so you don't have to try to tell who's successful or not)

It still doesn't change the fact that there really aren't very many "coaches" out there who really are amazing and are helping their clients get astounding results. There are even fewer who are great at coaching AND make a healthy living as they run a coaching business.

Here's the two reasons why:

- Most coaches are good at their craft OR their set of expertise. They *aren't* good at business… particularly marketing! (and most of them don't enjoy it either). **This means they don't have enough**

---

2 https://becomeacareercoach.com/certification

- people who are interested in their services to survive!
- Most coaches don't charge enough for their services to make a healthy living. **This means they don't know how to value the result they are providing OR aren't focused on providing a particular result.**

Let's call this group of well-intentioned people who aren't getting paid what they are worth and not helping very many people the "Broke Coaches." I want to help you become a successful coach with a thriving business because it helps the entire coaching profession and people who are working with coaches.

Here's what Broke Coaches are doing that you don't want to and (shouldn't need to) do.

Trying to be Everywhere

Broke Coaches are on Instagram, LinkedIn, Snapchat, Facebook, Twitter, Foursquare (wait is Foursquare still around!) and whatever the latest type of social media that Gary Vaynerchuk has mentioned might be hot in the future.

They are chasing after people EVERYWHERE.

I don't know about you, but I did this for like two weeks and it was exhausting. Plus, my mind always goes to the question of "how do you make this easy?" and possibly even fun!!!

To be clear, there are a couple people I have seen this work for. Those people are extremely intentional with their strategy and they LOVE social media. Personally, this isn't for me; I would rather be helping people by coaching them than spending my time that way.

On top of this, these same people are writing blog posts, and publishing articles on LinkedIn and, wait, maybe I should be starting a YouTube channel... and what about my new podcast? It got three downloads today.

Ughh... I'm exhausted again.

You can stop doing this. Right now. Stop! Yes, I know people tell you to do this. Don't listen. It's a recipe for disaster.

When you've done so well that you can hire other people to support your business (can anyone say "executive assistant please!!!"), then you can be in more places! It's a much shorter road than you would think!

Until then, you have permission not to "be everywhere."

Trying to help everyone

I'm warning you right now. This one will be hard for you.

It's been hard for each person I've helped become a career coach. It was difficult for me too.

Everyone goes through this learning curve. I hope to help you go through it faster.

The type of people who make great coaches are generally the type of people who truly enjoy helping others.

This means that Broke Coaches make the mistake of not focusing on one very, very specific target market (or very specific type of people with a specific type of problem they can solve). Instead, you get "life coaches" and very general coaches who are afraid to exclude anybody.

This, of course, means that they don't really appeal to anybody and don't really get to help out.

The irony here is that it works backwards from how most people think.

When you start very specific, it causes you to stand out and appeal to a targeted group. Then people want your help with many different problems instead of just the problem that they came to you for.

However, if you start the way Broke Coaches start, then you are trying to appeal to everyone and then people are confused about what you do and if you're the right person to help them.

This of course leads to binging on hazelnut dark chocolate (mmm…) and crying in a corner wondering why this coaching thing is so hard and if you're really meant to be a coach.

Don't do that. Stop it. Before you even start! Later on in this guide I will show you some examples of how specific you need to be with your target market. This will help you reach people in a way that they feel like you understand them and have a connection with them (and truly you will). Keep reading to learn how.

The prettiest website wins (or does it?)

I've had so many emails from people who have spent a ton of time or money developing a beautiful, professional-looking website. Or spending tons of time with their business license or choosing the right accounting software or trying to get everything just right for when clients come in the door!

Jennifer  4/24/15
to me

Hey Scott,

I hope all is well in your world…and that your business continues to thrive! I'm reaching out to you, as well as some other professionals, for some insight and perspective on what steps I should be taking to grow my business. With my website launched, I'm left wondering what are other ways I can grow my client base…and what should I be doing right now to make that happen??

I opened my business account this morning, and I still have the tasks of creating my spreadsheets for accounting/coaching hours/etc. From your entrepreneurial experience, do you have any lessons learned or guidance you can offer which may help me further develop

I am all ears!!

Thanks so much for your time,

----Jen----

When I ask these same people how many clients they have, the answer is either:

> none yet OR

> I have a few people that are unpaid.

For some reason, we associate the appearances of success with feeling like we are successful. Which means that too many of us spend a ridiculous amount of time on things like our websites making it look like we have lots of clients, when we could spend that same time just going and getting lots of clients.

I've done it too! That's how I learned Wordpress — by spending over 30 hours trying unsuccessfully to make my website look "professional."

We teach people in our Coaching Training programs how to put together a very simple but effective website and exactly what parts you actually need versus which parts are a waste of time when you're starting. Here's the secret. It's not much!

Later on in this guide, we'll actually show you how to attract leads from people who want to work with you WITHOUT a website. Crazy right?

Not really. What's crazy is spending a ton of time and money to get spreadsheets ready for clients you don't even have!

Stop doing this. It's distracting you from the part of the business where you help people and make money by helping people! Plus it's what Broke Coaches do!

Here's a short list of other things you can stop doing. You have our permission! Somebody else telling you to do them? I'll write you an "excused note" saying you don't have to. Just email me!

- Stop trying to be on all places at once (you don't need to be on all social media channels. Hang out where your people are.)

- Stop messing around with your website (it's never finished even when you run a six- or seven-figure business).

The question people always ask:

How do I start? What should I do first?

A far better question:

What do I not need to do? What are the few things that matter more than anything else?

What holds most career coaches back is thinking that they need to do everything. If not everything, then we often find that coaches are focused on the wrong things. There are very few things that you need to do and only a few actions that will help you more than anything else. Give yourself permission to NOT have to do everything and instead ask what matters more than anything else.

Also that's what we'll talk about in the next chapter!

How Do I Learn to Run a Business

If you've ever attended a university, gone to class at a high school, or have ever known anyone who went to kindergarten or nursery school, then you have an idea how average education works.

Typically you have a subject area like science or geometry and then you learn everything about that subject area that's deemed appropriate for your class or grade level. For geometry, that might mean you learn about lines, planes, angles, parallel lines, triangles, similarity, trigonometry, quadrilaterals, transformations, circles and area.

You learn all of this regardless of whether you will ever use it in the future. This includes both in future classes as well as in the "real world."

Of course, you could make the argument that everyone needs to be able to calculate the area of an isosceles triangle; if so, you and I would have to agree to disagree.

Regardless of where you stand on the need for triangles and quadrilaterals in daily life, I think we can all agree that one thing is true:

Top-performers in any industry craft or area approach learning in a completely different way than the rest of the world.

Instead of the ways that many of us were shown through the general education system, they follow two rules when learning new information or skills.

1) Top-performers focus on a specific goal or need

For example: If I am learning to play piano, I want to evaluate what I really want out of it. Do I really want to know everything about piano? Or is there something else more important?

After a parents-forced stint as a young child at learning the piano for a year, I decided I was interested again. I could have gone the "normal educational route," but I really had no desire to play *Twinkle Twinkle Little Star* and all of the other songs that you learn when you start to play piano.

As I evaluated what was most important to me, I realized that all I really wanted was to learn a few songs in particular.

I wanted to be able to sit down at the piano at a hotel or a friend's house and bust out John Legend's *All of Me*. So I set my goal at learning that and two other songs that I wanted to be able to play for the rest of my life.

This meant I didn't have to learn the "Every Good Boy Does Fine" or take the time to learn the skill of reading music for piano and, instead, I could focus on the most effective way for me to learn those songs.

That brings us to step number two that all top-performers use to learn.

2) After you have defined the goal, what is the shortest or most effective way to make it happen?

For me, if all I wanted to know was those three songs, then I needed to focus on the shortest ways to learn them.

Even if I personally didn't know what those were, I could ask my piano-playing friends that knew way more than me what to focus on if I just wanted to learn these songs.

It turns out all I needed was several tutorial videos on YouTube and about 10 minutes of practice time a day.

This would have been impossible without first defining what I really actually wanted to learn in the first place.

So, if your goal is to become a career coach or build a coaching business, you won't need to learn EVERYTHING. (That's impossible and setting you up for failure.)

Let's practice this right now (because you might as well have this help you immediately).

What are just the 1-3 things that you most need to learn to be successful in this area.

Here are just a few areas that I believe people need to learn to run a coaching business.

- How to create a powerful and effective coaching conversation that is so useful your potential clients can't help but want more.
- How to sell coaching organically by using coaching techniques to help your potential clients.
- Learning to understand someone's deepest needs (for the purposes of both coaching and market research)
- Crafting a message that stands out and moves people emotionally.

Notice how specific all of these are. The more specific you can be the easier and shorter the learning process will be. Take a few moments and write down what you feel like you need and want to learn most to run a coaching business then keep reading to get a head start on how to learn them!

The question people always ask:

How do I learn to become a career coach?

A far better question:

How do I learn to learn more effectively?

Once you've learned to structure your learning, it becomes much easier to do anything that you want to. You'll start to recognize what pieces you need to learn most and what pieces aren't helping you with your goal. Everything becomes much more possible when you approach learning like this, including building a career-coaching business!

How Do I Sell Coaching?

MANY YEARS AGO, I used to teach sales classes with all different types of advanced techniques and sales closes.

We'd cover things like soft closes versus hard closes or the stonewall technique and objection handling.

I found the psychology of sales and why someone says "yes" rather than "no" fascinating.

For example, did you know that when I used to work as a contractor running a residential painting business, more people would say yes when I would accept their offer of coffee rather than declining it?

It's not for the reason you'd think either. It turns out that me engaging in similar behavior to their own in their own home made them feel more comfortable with me, and therefore more likeable. Even more importantly this simple act of graciously accepting their offer of a beverage and taking the time to consume it with them, made them feel that I enjoyed and appreciated them.

In other words it wasn't just that they liked me, it was that they felt that I liked them that caused them to want to work with me and my team of painting professionals at the time.

I'm a total nerd for the science behind why we choose to buy from somehow, however , I've learned that no matter how you feel about psychology, "sales closes," or coffee, none of those are actually required to sell coaching.

Let me repeat that:

You don't need to know fancy sales closes and techniques to sell coaching.

You can learn to successfully sell coaching and do so ethically and organically, but not unless you first learn the principles of great selling.

If you go right to techniques or tactics, and straight into trying to close the sale all the time, then you become just like the used car salesman who everyone knows and loves to hate.

You know the one. He's got slicked-back hair, maybe a creeper moustache, and he's wearing a slightly wrinkled button-down shirt with the top unbuttoned so that you can see his sweet gold chain hanging around his neck. Everybody has met this guy! He probably has a name like Gino or something.

I don't want you to be like him. He's the epitome of bad sales. He uses high-pressure tactics, he doesn't care all that much about what you're really looking for, and what you need, just about making the sale.

I have seen some of the nicest people accidentally turn into Gino, because they think sales has to "look" a certain way.

Or people get really nervous about sales because they feel awkward about presenting coaching as a valuable service and charging money for it.

Selling coaching is far easier than you might imagine because the easiest way to sell coaching is to allow people to experience it.

The experience of really mind-blowing, powerful coaching is something that no explanation can replace. No description of coaching is a substitute for going through a life-changing coaching conversation.

This is great news, because instead of focusing on selling someone, you can instead focus on helping in the very best way possible!

What's even better is that you can focus all your efforts on becoming an amazing coach because that will make you better at getting clients.

Here's how this can work for you in reality.

One of the students in our Professional Career Coach training program was nervous about whether or not she could sell coaching, even though she hadn't yet been certified.

She had already been helping several people by coaching them to "practice" and each of them was absolutely loving the coaching she was doing with them.

This, of course, was because they had already experienced the power of coaching.

I asked her why she wasn't yet working with them as paying clients and she said she was unsure how to transition to the conversation about money.

I asked her to share this with each person as she was wrapping up their "practice coaching engagement":

"It seems like you've been getting quite a bit out of our coaching together. Would you like to keep working with me? If you have what everything need, let's end our work together here. But if you'd like to continue to work with me, I'd be thrilled to schedule a conversation with you where we discuss exactly how I can help from here and exactly what that would look like, including the cost of investment. Is that something you'd like to do?"

She went and had that conversation and just days later had her first paying client.

Here's why it worked:

It drew clear boundaries about where the free coaching started and stopped.

It's important to be clear and up front with this. If you don't value your time (and theirs), your clients won't either.

This verbiage was also very organic. It addressed, head-on, the logical next step and progression in the coaching relationship.

It also provided help and service by asking, "is that something you'd like to do?"

Lastly, it gave them the option. There was no forcing them to have an additional conversation, no asking them to pay you for things they don't find valuable or helpful. It was simply asking if they wanted to have a conversation to learn what it would take to work with you.

This type of help and support provides the very best way to serve.

Serving is the equivalent of great sales experiences.

Also one very important element that is lost upon many new coaches is that, at this point in the conversation, they have said "yes" they want to know how to work with you. They've asked you for it. You haven't forced them into it at all.

This means that, during that next conversation, you can communicate your offer with ease *because they have asked you to.*

Here's what that might sound like coming from a coach who's had a little bit of practice:

"I charge $6,000 to work with clients for four months. During this time, I will help you clarify your wants and strengths, identify places you're best-suited to leverage those, and build a plan to make your career change. Is this what you're looking for?"

I've personally worked with many new career coaches and we have customized how they meet, interact, and converse with new clients. However, I've found that most new coaches benefit from this simple process that breaks down interactions with new clients.

It looks like this:

Step 1 is recognizing the opportunity and learning how to respond to those opportunities whenever and wherever they pop up.

Step 2 is inviting the low-hanging fruit to have a conversation to get help from you. This is a simple invite. You are putting it out there for them to say "Yes" and for you to gain their permission that they do, in fact, want help. Often, this will come after you've had a very short conversation with them, and they have expressed that they are having some sort of challenge in their career.

Step 3 is having the coaching conversation to learn their needs, struggles, and wants and giving them specific help for free. Then, you pivot into step 4 if they want it.

Step 4 is where you invite them to schedule a separate "sales call." This is where you discuss exactly what the path would be, the details of working together, and how you would help going forward. Then ask if they'd like to work with you, and if they do, accept money or set up follow up.

That's the entire process in a nutshell.

Now, let's break each step down in more detail.

Step 1 is recognizing the opportunity. You likely have opportunities that are right in front of you or nearby, but you may not recognize them yet. These might be people who you've worked with in the past, or people you interact with who go to the same clubs or workout facilities. They may be parents of kids that play sports with your kids or go to the same schools or events, or maybe they even play your sports or go to your events. It could even be the person in front of you in the line for coffee.

Taking the time to plant this seed helps bring it to the front of your mind and enable you to see opportunities that have always been there in a new light. Everything you need is already right in front of you.

Ironically, it functions the same way as when you go buy a new SUV in a certain color, like silver, and then you start to see that same silver SUV everywhere. It feels like there are tons of them, but the reality is you just didn't recognize them before.

The cause of this is your brain filtering information in, rather than what it used to do, which was filtering that same info out. Up until you bought a silver Ford Explorer, it considered this info to be irrelevant. This cognitive bias can be used for intentional good rather than just random SUV sightings.

Our goal is to begin training your brain to "filter in" and recognize those opportunities to help others in a coaching capacity.

Also, later we will cover some more proactive methods like creating simple speaking engagements or relationship-building opportunities. But for now, I want you to realize those aren't a requirement.

When you create the opportunity, we want you to be ready to invite that individual to a conversation. This is step 2.

This invitation can be very, very simple. Here's how it might sound if they say, "I'm thinking about getting into a new career, but I haven't decided if that's something I actually want to do or not."

Your invitation may sound like:

> *"Oh really? That's actually something that I do. I help people get into different careers, make career changes, or help them with their career. I'd love to hear more."*

Then allow them to tell you more. At that point in time, you can simply invite them to a conversation and say,

> *"You know, I'd be thrilled to help you out with that if you're interested. I'd be happy to have a*

conversation with you, help as much as I can during the conversation, and then, if you decide you want more help beyond than that, we can talk about that at that point in time. That (Then insert their problem and challenge) is something I help people with. It sounds like you might benefit from that. Would you be interested in scheduling a 60-minute conversation? There's no obligation."

The goal of this first conversation is to help, serve, build trust and relationship. It allows them to experience coaching and sample the goods before they decide that YES this is exactly what they want and need.

The goal of conversation 2 is for you to have a separate "sales call," as we discussed earlier. When you separate out the two, it becomes much more clear who really wants help and is willing to pay you for it. Also, they have an understanding of exactly how they get help, so there are fewer objections or questions because you've already demonstrated it for them.

In this lesson, you learned the 5-step process for converting low-hanging fruit into prospects. This process included: Step 1: Recognize the opportunity and respond. Step 2: Invite them to have a conversation and get help from you. Step 3: Learn their needs, struggles, and wants in a free coaching conversation. Step 4: Invite them to schedule a separate sales call, Step 5: Sign them up or ask if they are moving forward.

In the next lesson, we will cover how to specifically have that coaching conversation and how to organically pivot to a sales conversation that they want to have because you've already started helping them.

This may be as simple as saying "I'd love to help, want to hop on the phone and you can tell me more about what you're looking for?"

Then coordinate a time to do exactly that.

The question people always ask:

How do I sell coaching?

A far better question:

How do I provide my potential clients so much help they can't not work with me?

The very best way to have people understand the value of coaching is when they have experienced how powerful it can be firsthand. This means that helping them by coaching them is the most effective way to sell coaching.

Where Do I Find Coaching Clients?

There's this secret to marketing success. Only it's not really a secret.

It's actually more like great advice that nobody really actually does, because they don't see the value in it.

It's like when you borrow your Dad's truck and it's slick out and he warns you that it's really slick and that you will have to go really, really slow and drive differently than you normally do and you shrug it off and say "I know, I know," but then less than five minutes later you've run the truck into a dumpster and you can't quite figure out how it happened.

You know the feeling...Wait. You've never done that?

Oh... me neither!

Anyhow, it's this thing that most people know they're supposed to do and they give it lip service but never really do it and then wonder why it's so hard to figure out what you should be doing to grow your business.

What is this big "non-secret" that is the business equivalent of exercising and eating right to keep from being fat?

It's called your "target market"... also called your niche, ideal audience, avatar, target customer, and your "wheezy" (ok, I made up that last one!).

Whatever you call it, one thing is true. Everyone underestimates the power of this.

Here's a comparison of the difference between the Broke Coach and a profitable coach making six figures from her business.

	Broke Coach (Career Coach)	**Olivia Gamber (my former client)**
Target Market (when starting out)	Women 20-50, who want to change jobs	Women 26-32. Highly educated, with a master's or PH.D, underemployed millennials making 50-60k, Live in the USA, with 1 or more jobs. On the job hunt right now and not having success.

Where Do I Find Coaching Clients?

	Broke Coach (Career Coach)	Olivia Gamber (my former client)
What do they want?	They want a really good job that pays them more money.	They want to feel like their education was worth it; they want to feel like their talents are not going to waste in a job that's beneath them.
Why do they want it?	Uhhh... Not totally sure?	They feel like they are wasting their time and their lives. They want to contribute to something. They want to feel like their parents can be proud of them and not afraid to tell people about what they do. They want to be challenged.
What are their fears/ frustrations?	They are worried they will not reach their full potential in their career.	They are embarrassed to be doing work that doesn't need an advanced degree, they are barely making money after the student loan payment. They worry the investment in grad school was a waste.

Ok, the difference between how well they know their market is obvious. Great. Whatever...

The real question is: 'What does knowing your Target Market actually do for you?'

I'm so glad you asked!!!

Well, aside from the extremely obvious piece that if you know exactly what the people in your market are thinking before they even think it, then it makes it incredibly easy to communicate with them.

Which of course means:

> When you create an offer for them, you know exactly what they are really looking for!

- It allows you to know what types of incredibly helpful content you can create for them that is going to have them looking to you as the authority in their eyes. (without any guesswork) More on this in the Client Attraction Magnet section.

- By the time you get on a "sales call" with them, you don't have to do any "Used Car Lot" tactics because it just becomes about giving them what you already know they need and nothing else.

More importantly than all of that, it helps you know exactly where they hang out.

When you know exactly where they are, you can just go to where they are.

Wait, that was so simple, you might have missed it. Let me say it again.

When you know where the exact people who have the exact problem you solve spend their time, you can go right to them!

Here's how to think about this differently. Remember that the Broke Coach is wandering around going crazy trying to be everywhere. Well, this is the exact reason why!

If I know exactly the person I'm trying to reach, I would know where they spend their time. And why would I keep interacting with everyone on LinkedIn, Twitter, and Facebook if my target market spends the majority of their time on Instagram?

Don't answer that! Rhetorical question. Besides, you already know the answer and can probably feel the relief rolling over you that you don't have to do all this "extra" stuff.

When you're running around doing everything and not focused on a very specific person, your efforts can't be concentrated AT ALL.

You've heard the analogy of throwing a pebble into the ocean. You know it doesn't do much!

I don't want you doing that. I don't even want you throwing your marketing pebbles into a lake... or even a pond!

No. Instead, I want you throwing a boulder into a stream! A stream of ultra-specific people who you already know are going to respond to your message.

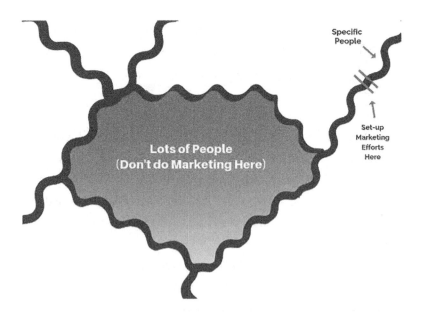

Here's an example of how some of our students have decided and found their target market. what that looks like:

I met Susan when she enrolled in the Business Accelerator track of our Professional Career Coaching Program.

She suspected she might want to work with spouses or partners of military service people primarily because she had been that person before and felt she had an understanding of that market.

NOTE: We very often find ourselves recommending to our students that they start with a market they already have familiarity with. It shortens the learning curve and it enables you to quickly build a deeper level relationship later on if you have "been there" in one way or another. We also encounter a lot of people that attempt to pick markets that they're not familiar with at all. - This means you if you're 3 years out of college but want to work 50+ executives in their second act career just because many of those people can afford to pay higher coaching prices.

Spoiler Alert: This is an uphill battle because even if you have done all the extra work to get familiar with a market you have no experience with, those people may find it more difficult to be comfortable with someone who's never been remotely close to their situation. It's not impossible, but why stack the odds against you when you're starting out. Choose an initial market you've belonged to in the past or have familiarity with.

This is what Susan did with US military spouses.

Since had been one herself, she knew some people that fell into this group. This meant that when she wanted to learn more about this target market those people that were already in her network were the first people she reached out to have "research" conversations with.

She contacted them by Facebook messenger (but you can also do this with phone or email or LinkedIn) and let them know that she was starting a new business and was doing market research. She would go onto share that she felt they might fit into her target market and was wondering if she could ask them some questions about how they think about some of their career problems.

More often than not people are thrilled that you asked and excited to help. This allowed Susan to have a conversation to learn more about the people in her market.

Keep in mind this is NOT a conversation where you tell them all about the services that you offer. Instead your opportunity here is to learn about them, how they think about the challenges in their life and career right now? what is stopping them from getting what they want? What are the specific words and verbiage they use to describe all of it? and of course try to learn "where they hang out?" in other words where do they spend their time?

These conversations take a bit of practice because much like coaching itself, it requires open ended questions that don't lead people along. It requires true listening and genuine interest in them to get the information you need without accidentally influencing it.

Here's some examples of great questions that you can use during this conversation:

- What are some of your current career goals (the ones you actually care most about?)
- What do you feel like is stopping you from reaching those goals?
- What do you want out of your career that hasn't yet panned out the way you thought it would?
- What types of blogs, websites, podcasts, magazines, etc do you read/listen to? (where do you go for help, advice, entertainment? - You can often preface this question and share something like "I'm trying to learn more about where people like you spend their time that I might be able to later reach them")

Here's some examples of bad questions that you shouldn't go near because they won't be helpful to you:

- Do you think you would buy coaching?
- Do you know what career coaching is?
- How much would you pay for coaching?

- Do you think that if you were changing careers you would go to a coach?
- Would you please be my client?

There's always one person who will read this and think "Isn't it just better to ask them directly? Why do I have to beat around the bush?" And then they proceed with asking these questions and they get answers that seem helpful at first.

Until they realize that when you ask these types of questions, they unitentionally lead people along a path. These people want to help you which often translates to sharing the answer they think you want to hear.

That's not helpful to you. Resist the urge and start the conversation by sharing that I'd love to ask you a variety of questions about how you think about your career and what you're working on. There's no right answers except those that are true for you and the very best way you can help me is by sharing those instead of what you might think I want to hear. I really want to know what's true for you.

Susan was able to do this. She learned that many of the challenges that she faced as a Military spouse were similar to what she experienced. Challenges like "wanting to find flexibility in location" because they wanted to have a career AND support their service people.

These conversations validated that what she suspected she knew about the market was true and there was a real need there that coaching could help with.

Additionally though she realized that there are A LOT of ways to reach military spouses. One example of this was Facebook groups that they already belonged to and were actively engaged and participating in.

One thing I've learned is that many people expect this part to be easy. It's not, but it always seems obvious after the fact!

"Of course Military spouses are involved in Facebook groups"

Except that realization comes with doing the research and having those conversations and beginning to put together tidbits about what you know about your market. Those tidbits connect you to a small realization, then another and another.

Sometimes this can feel a little like CSI style detective work. It's often not easy but the realizations about where to reach your target market were worth it in Susan's case and every other person that we've worked with.

Once you know where these people are, you can simply go to where they are at and, at first, you can throw your boulder in that stream. But later on as you build authority and credibility in that space, I want you building a dam on that stream!

Now regardless of how you feel about the ecological effects of big dams on tiny little streams, we can all agree that going upstream and plunking yourself down right where you know those people will be coming is a way better approach than chasing after them wherever they might go in the big ocean!

Again though! I would rather be strategic and fun rather than spending large portions of my life being frustrated.

Once you're there in front of that stream, you need to know what to offer them, so that they want to stop and spend their time with you, rather than keep on swimming toward the ocean!

And that is what we cover in the next section.

The question people always ask:

Where do I find coaching clients?

A far better question:

How do I decide who I want to work with?

Once you've decided who you want to work with, then you can go and talk to them. You can learn everything about them and then you'll have the answers to where and how to reach people in your target market.

How Do I Package a Coaching Offer?

If I say the word offer, there is a massive difference in what the craft coach thinks versus what a successful profitable coach thinks of.

Here's what pops out when I ask the Broke Coach that question about "what's your offer?"

"Oh… I uh… I give them six Skype sessions with me for $697."

Then I guess I must stare at them in disbelief for a moment because it's always followed by something like, "but I was thinking about doing an 8-session package for $997 and raising my prices a bit."

We tend to think about an offer as the "stuff" we are giving them, OR the time we are spending with them.

That's one direction you could go. Which is better than going nowhere I suppose.

If you choose to, you can trudge down that painfully long winding road to profitless transactions that empty out your heart and cause you to question if you're really cut out for "helping others."

And if you like that sort of painful despair, by all means, keep on going down that road. Please!

If you're not the sort of person who likes running headlong into a wall again and again, let me propose a different way.

What if instead you sold outcomes or results? Because that's what people are really buying anyway. Or in the case of the Broke Coach; not buying!

Let me give you an example of how this works.

At the end of 2016, my family and I went to Portugal and Paris for about six weeks. While I was there, we really badly wanted to climb up the bell tower in Notre Dame Cathedral in the heart of Paris.

Even though it was winter (the offseason), we found ourselves standing in a very long line in the coldest season in France (primarily because only 20 people can go up the narrow circular staircase at a time).

How Do I Package a Coaching Offer?

Across the street from the bell tower line were three little shops. One offered hats and gloves of all kinds. Another offered warm drinks and crepes, and still another offered all varieties of tourist crap (Eiffel towers and keychains in any size as you can imagine!).

We stood there for all of 20 minutes talking before the cold began to sink in and my kids began to get restless.

The warm drink vendor across the way all of a sudden began to look very appealing. I didn't even want something to drink when I got there and honestly wasn't in the mood for Chocolat Chaud (Hot Chocolate) or the Vin

Chaud (French Hot Spiced Wine that, when the French pronounce it, sounds much like "von chow").

As the time passed and we grew colder and our kids started running through the legs of the very nice English couple behind us, we decided it was definitely time for some hot chocolate and mulled wine!

So I crossed the street and paid a ridiculous number of Euros for five teeny cups!

Now why did I do that? I knew it was overpriced. I knew exactly what was going on.

I didn't care about the drinks. In fact I didn't even want the drinks!

I happily paid the man in the chocolat chaud tent because it solved my problem!

If you remember from that last section — the very best way to have customers fall into your lap is to stay away from the ocean and instead to find the tiny little stream with the exact people who have the exact problem you can solve.

Those street vendors weren't offering a cup of Hot Chocolate or Vin Chaud. The offer was instead to "get warm" and enjoy doing it.

How Do I Package a Coaching Offer?

For me, it solved my problem of keeping my three little kids occupied and having their little hands warmed up. And me feeling like a good parent versus subjecting my kids to the cold for 90 minutes only to walk up 720 stairs to the top to look at stone gargoyles and a foggy Eiffel tower (which was still awesome BTW!).

I wanted to solve these problems so badly that I didn't even care exactly how much it cost or what the exact form of packaging it was in. It was irrelevant (think; six Skype sessions for $697!).

When you are very aware of what value you deliver, you can charge based on that value NOT by the hour or any other way, and your target market will gladly pay you to help solve their problems.

From there it simply becomes a matter of testing the market and seeing what are the best price points. And remember when you're talking to people one at a time, it means every conversation you have is an opportunity to test what you have learned so far and see if it's accurate. This means you can do market testing in a matter of days sometimes!

So, what's an example of a great offer versus a less than great offer.

Crash Course on Salary Negotiation

12 Short Videos

Each video will teach you an essential skill in negotiations, and prepare you for your next big conversation.

Basic
FREE

5 Session E-Course

Helpful tips & tricks

Real-world case studies

Subscribe

now

Practical, Useful Exercises

I've created, tested, and optimized multiple exercises to help you discover, research, and practice to be a better negotiator.

Yes
$149.00 USD

Basic Plan

One Year Unlimited Course Access

Two 30-minute consultations with Heather

Select

1-1 Consulting Included!

In a 1:1 consultation with me, I will teach you a collaborative framework for negotiating and give you strategies to confidently ask for what you want.

Heck Yes!
$449.00 USD

Premium Plan

One Year Unlimited Course Access

Four 30 minute consultations with Heather

Join

now

What's wrong with this offer?

Nobody (except me and I'm a weirdo) wants to be a better negotiator for negotiations sake.

Instead, they want a particular outcome. In this case, they want to get paid a larger salary. Why do they want to get paid a larger salary? Depends on the market, but it may be any of the following problems they need solved!

- Want to feel like they are getting compensated fairly for the work they do.
- Want to feel like they're taken seriously in their job or they're valuable to the company.
- Want to get college debt paid off.
- Their current life isn't fitting the lifestyle they envisioned.
- Or many more problems!

No matter what it is, this offer isn't focused on any of those! Instead it's only focused on the tool itself (negotiation).

That means the person in this target market must spell out for themselves how negotiation coaching is going to help solve their problems, and if you aren't making it easy for them, it often leads to confusion.

Confused potential customers don't buy! Even if you can actually help!

This offer could go from mediocre to great simply by focusing on the particular results or outcome that this target market wants — i.e. What does the negotiation actually get them (the problem for them that it solves)?

Now here's the catch!

One target market might have a different reason for solving this problem than another, which is why it's so important that you focus very narrowly at first. You can then speak their language!

If I'm focused only on helping 30-year-old administrative assistants with a college degree or advanced degree get paid more, it may be because they feel they are undervalued and underpaid and with a hint of embarrassment because they feel underemployed.

However, if it's 45+ executives that I'm helping negotiate, there is a whole different set of reasons behind why they want to get paid more.

No matter what, I want to understand and be able to communicate those when I make them an offer.

However, there's an even bigger reason why I might be interested in understanding exactly what they want and need. It's what will allow you to get in front of them in the first place, AND cause them to want to talk to you, AND already believe that you can help them!

Want to know how to do that?

Well then keep reading, it's exactly what we talk about in the next section!

How to Attract People by Allowing Them to Self-select

Most coaches who want to have a "digital presence" want to jump right into this piece!

I can't tell you how many coaches I've talked to that have already started creating an e-book, or video series, or even writing an actual book without understanding who it is that they're talking to, OR what these people actually want and how you can help (your offer!).

The rest of the coaches and consultants that haven't already started blindly creating something are instead left wondering "What should I do?"

Eventually, they decide on a video series or something else without ever knowing if that's what is going to work well. So they go through the trouble to make it and find out it was a bad idea in the first place.

Now if you already know your target market, who they are and what they want and need, you already have the information to answer these questions, but with a much higher degree of accuracy than our Broke Coaches.

I'll show you how this works, but first let's define what a Client Attraction Magnet is and why you would want to create one.

How to get people to raise their hand to say they're interested in working with you

I've focused a lot of my business on spending my time with the people who are excited to work with me and who I can help — and ignoring the rest.

This is exactly one of the biggest reasons to create a solid client attraction magnet.

Think about it:

If you had a way to automatically (without spending your time) separate everyone you would be excited to work with from the rest of the crowd, wouldn't you do it?

But wait it gets better. These same people *want to give you explicit permission* to build a relationship with them and have you send them things that build you up as an authority in their eyes so they begin to trust you!

You might think, ok who am I going to have to bribe to make this happen?

But that's the beauty of it. You can do all of this without being manipulative or deceiving by using a Client Attraction Magnet!

What is a Client Attraction Magnet?

A Client Attraction Magnet is also called a Lead Magnet, an Opt-in Gift as well as many other names.

Is an ethical bribe that offers something of value to someone in your target market that is given in exchange for their contact information.

A more simple explanation of how this works: You have something valuable to me (like information that helps me get a raise) and I happily give you my contact info in order to get it.

Client attraction magnets come in many forms:
- Video series
- Checklist

- Swipe files
- Webinars
- E books (and regular books)
- Guides
- Mini courses (or full courses)
- Free membership
- And many more...

As I mentioned earlier, Broke Coaches get really caught up in the modality of their Client Attraction Magnet. Profitable coaches realize that it's much more important to solve a particular problem or give a specific chunk of value that will help separate the people in your Target Market from everyone else!

You've already done the work for this at this point too, so all you have to do is look at what your target wants and needs.

The very best magnets will solve a smaller problem or a chunk of the bigger problem that your ideal client has, OR it will help them understand the path to solving the bigger problem (and maybe even think about it in a different way!).

Here's some examples of Client Attraction Magnets that we use for ourselves.

FigureItOut.co[3] — Figure it Out 8-Day Mini Course

At first glance, this may not look like much (and there isn't much there), but this is one of many versions that we've tested.

This is targeted toward a very specific group of people. They use this verbiage "work that fits" when they describe what they want.

Their Problem: They are in jobs that they don't find desirable and feel they are meant for something better. They want to stop wasting time and finally figure out what they should do for their career. They are tired of not having this answer and feel like it's stopping them from truly living their life.

---

3   http://figureitout.co

In short, they are in the wrong job and want to understand what they should be doing for their career to have work they enjoy and which fits their lifestyle. They're looking for an answer.

What does this Client Attraction Magnet do for them?

It helps them understand chunks of a process they can use to solve their problem. Some people can go through the entire process and have their solution and not even have to pay for it (which, by the way, is a good thing; those people share it and spread the word!).

Other people get an understanding of the process they will need to go through to solve their problem. This can be just as valuable to them — to "see the pathway" — as it is to walk down the path. Because it now gives them hope.

What is it actually? (How does it work behind the scenes)

It's a series of emails delivered from an email service provider like Mailchimp.[4] On each day of the 8 days, they get that email with a link to a blog post on our website using Wordpress through a "hosted" website

---

4   http://happentoyourcareer.com/mailchimp

(we use BlueHost[5] for many of our sites and it is a great starter solution).

When someone self-selects to "opt in" to the page (pictured above), they will be added to our email list and then be sent emails similar to the one below which each provide a link in the email to a webpage with a video and a short set of actions for them to take.

Make a Decision

"If you want to make a difference, make a decision!" -Eric Thomas

It's up to you now! We've done all we can do to get you on the path to the job that you love. All that is left is to decide to take the next step.

Voila!! Video course! BTW, for more info on how to set up a website or some of the other tools we recommend you can find instructions here.[6]

---

5   http://happentoyourcareer.com/bluehost
6   http://www.happentoyourcareer.com/how-to-create-a-wordpress-website-for-an-online-business-or-blog/

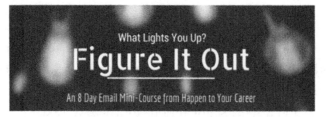

Here's another completely different take on a lead magnet. This is from David Mariano at FinanceCareerLaunch.com.[7] We helped him get his business started and get some of his first customers in 2016.

Instead of an ebook or a course or a video, he offers a membership site that houses several of these items for his target audience and the people who subscribe to his email list. They often find him from a google search about Finance Careers or from his Finance Podcast and from there visit his website (we'll discuss examples of how to do this in our chapter on "creating traffic"). Once

---

7   http://financecareerlaunch.com/

they are on his website those people see his CAM and some of them give him their email and he gives them a username and password to access all of the many resources he has on the site.

If you're just starting out often beginning with a simple client attraction magnet will move you faster. This is an advanced option and certainly not right for every target market, but helps you understand a non-traditional take on the subject! He's created the go-to set of resources for would-be finance professionals wanting to advance their careers.

Each Stage of Your Career Requires a Boost, a Launch Strategy

INITIAL LAUNCH	RELAUNCH	ACCELERATION
Foundation	Career Change	Expand Your Influence
How to set yourself apart. Build the mindsets, habits and skills of the most successful businesspeople.	Get unstuck and break into the finance career you love (even without the "ideal" experience).	How to build relationships and win clients with new media and time-tested principles.

GET FREE ACCESS

Here's some questions to ask when getting ready to create a Client Attraction Magnet

How does your target market like to consume content?

This will help you decide what modality might be best for them (Ebook vs. video vs. something else).

What are the smaller problems that you can solve immediately for them?

These are often precursor or prerequisite problems that lead them further down the path to get where they want to go.

For example, if you coach people on nutrition and particularly smoothie diets, you may be able to provide detailed reviews of juicers or machines to make smoothies. As you help them decide whether to get a Ninja or Kitchen Aid, you will be building trust with them so that you can later get the opportunity to help them further!

What can you do to deliver more value than you are comfortable with!

It should feel like you're giving away something that others might charge money for. This is part of what will cause people to want it, AND cause you to stand out at the same time!

Feel free to give away the farm. If you are doing coaching, most people will need more than just information from you to make the change! (Example: Most people charge for the info that's in this guide. I would prefer just to give it to you. We know that some of you will take it and run with it and we will get the opportunity to help others to work to implement all of it!)

How to Pull Off the Not-So-Magic Trick of Generating Traffic

All right! You've now got your Client Attraction Magnet, and you can describe the people in your target market better than they can, and you just plunk yourself down and wait now right?

Well not exactly!

There's one more piece of the puzzle here: Traffic.

What on earth is 'traffic' really?

Traffic, in this case, simply means bringing your Client Attraction Magnet to live human beings that likely need your help.

Where do you get these humans from? Do I need to shop local? Can I grow my own?

While I don't want to discourage you from raising mini-humans for the purposes of having them download your Client Attraction Magnet later on, there is a better way!

Remember everything you now know about your target market? All that work you did early on?

Well part of what you did was also learn where these people hang out, who they follow, what they click on. What websites and podcasts and blogs they pay attention to. Where do these people meet in real life?

Now this is where you get to use that info and plunk yourself down in one of those "streams" of your specific peeps!

There are several different ways.

The main ways I recommend are to Buy, Build, or Borrow.

Buying traffic (paying for peeps!)

Buying traffic usually means paid advertising. This can range from the ads you see on Facebook and Twitter, to sponsored blog posts, to buying sidebar ads on a website that happens to have your target market living there!

This method can work incredibly well, but let me start with two caveats:

- When we talk about buying ads to get peeps, we're not entering the realm of slave trade or something else creepy!

- This is usually not for beginners; you will want to be comfortable with establishing a budget that you may not see a return on at first before moving down this method!

Where can you do this?

- **Social Media:** Facebook, Twitter, LinkedIn, Instagram, etc.

- **Websites:** Ads, native advertising (messages that look like they are regular content).

- **Blogs:** Sponsored posts, side bars, headers, resource pages.

- **Search Engines:** Google AdWords, Google partners.

PROS	CONS
When done correctly, it's the fastest way to bring traffic to your Client Attraction Magnet. Some methods can expose you to extremely targeted audiences.	It requires both money AND an initial learning curve. You should not proceed unless you don't mind not getting an immediate return on your initial budget.

Building an audience

This is by far the crockpot method NOT the microwave method for traffic. It takes a lot of consistent action spread over time to build an audience in any one method.

To show you what I mean, here's the download numbers in a chart for one of our podcasts. We started this one from scratch (with no audience and no connections) This one has been running since late 2013. If you look closely, it really only began growing substantially in the last two years.

There are things you can do to speed this up, and I have a number of friends who have grown faster. However, I want you to understand that audience-building is a long-term strategy and usually works best when complemented with one of the other two options.

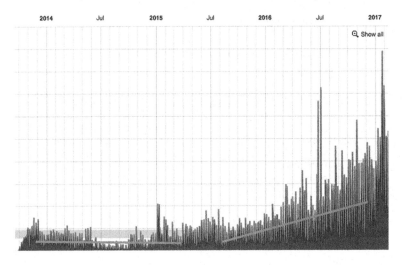

Here are some ways you can build an audience to bring traffic to your lead magnet. My team and I have experience in a lot of these areas, but we won't cover how to do these here since each one can be an entire class with multiple books to itself!

- Video-based shows or channels (Distributed on YouTube, Vimeo, or other places that act as search engines).

- Audio podcast or radio show (distributed on iTunes, Google Play, I Heart Radio, etc.).

- Blogs or writing-based feeds.

- Leveraging social media platforms' built-in options (Note: If you build an audience on social media, the disadvantage is that you don't own it and changes that platform makes can potentially affect you) Example: Facebook Live, Periscope, etc.

- Books (Distributed on Amazon for digital, or stores and online retailers for hard copy books).

PROS	CONS
Pros: In most cases listed above, you own the traffic or reason for the traffic. Also this is a way to bring continued and sustained leads to your business once you've gone through the initial effort of building an audience and it gains momentum.	**Cons:** It's slower than the other methods to get going and each option requires its own set of learning.

Borrowing traffic

This is where most people will get their initial traffic from besides their friends, Mom, and weird Aunt Susie who stays oddly up to date on everything you do (it's almost disturbing! ... And how does she know about that night with the tequila anyway!).

Anyhow, forget Aunt Susie, Here are some very specific ways you can borrow traffic from other existing audiences.

Contributed Writing — Contributing to an existing website or publishing company. For example, we contribute to TheMuse.com and Ramit Sethi's GrowthLab.com on a regular basis.

Guest Posts — Similar to contributed writing but specifically for those websites that are or have blogs. Often these are smaller but even more targeted than the publishing houses. We've written for EventualMillionaire.com, StartofHappiness.com and a number of others that have overlap with our target audiences!

Bonus: Here's my personal Evernote file with info on how to get to write guest posts and contributed articles.

https://www.evernote.com/l/AWztMM_kTCtP96MgtE36mziGjX4vHJI8d9o

Podcast Appearances — This is part of how I grew my audience AND found many clients. I went on over 100+ podcasts as a guest and I gave away "gifts" to their audience (my client attraction magnet, which was truly helpful for their audience!).

Bonus: Here's my personal Evernote file with info on good and bad pitch examples to be a guest on podcasts.

https://www.evernote.com/l/
AWyz-IawR5VAkaAEQiGAxUs6YhTMrWt-BdE

Media Appearances— This could be TV, radio, newspaper or other print. this is usually only worth your time if that "channel" has exposure to lots of people in your target market OR extremely high numbers in general!

Affiliate Relationships — Sometimes this might be referred to as affiliate marketing, joint ventures, or partnership marketing. These are other companies or people who are offering your client attraction magnet to their audience in exchange for a cut (commissions) on any product or service that you end up selling.

Just traffic from this approach alone has added over 10,000 people to our email list in the first three years of business.

Webinars or trainings for existing audiences — I have a friend who is a career development coach (for executives) and she regularly does webinar-style trainings for large recruiting firms.

Speaking and Workshops — This one deserves extra attention, just because it can be such an easy way to get clients at the very beginning of your business. In fact, this is how I got my very first coaching client (and my only local client to date!) I spoke at a young professional's function and collected $600 two days later! BOOM!

However, there's usually a longer (and more sustainable) road that you can use speaking for besides just your first client!

I helped one of my clients Kwame Christian, Negotiations Coach and Founder of AmericanNegotiationInstitute.com,[8] to his very first five-figure month by focusing on speaking at functions that had a captive audience in his target market. He would then capture emails from people who wanted his client attraction magnet by passing around an iPad (a clipboard works well here too if you don't mind manually entering emails!)

---

8   http://americannegotiationinstitute.com/

Another student who we've helped along the way is Michelle Robin from BrandYourCareer.com. She takes it a step further. One of her speaking presentations is called "Trash Your Resume." When she speaks, she passes around a trash can to collect everyone's business card and resumes from everyone who wants her Client Attraction Magnet. With this unique tactic, she will often have nearly the entire room wanting to maintain contact with her after she speaks!

PROS	CONS
Quickest and lowest-cost winners for traffic.	Disadvantage is many of these are one-time efforts with the exception of blog posts, which benefit from SEO and may get ongoing traffic. The rest of the methods require duplicating much of the effort to get the traffic each time.

How Put It on Autopilot

Systems are the best!

You don't have to think about it when you have a system. You don't have to waste precious time and energy when you have systems and best of all: When that system is automated, you don't even have to lift a finger to keep benefitting from it day in and day out!

We have some automated systems that we built years ago, that still, to this day, are making it easy for potential clients to get help, get to know us, and be prepped to buy from us — all without breaking a sweat (or even waking up for that matter!).

When you take the upfront time to build a system that delivers your client magnet, follows up on your behalf, AND even schedules potential clients to your calendar automatically, you have the ability to spend your time on other things!

You can focus on making sure your current clients are extremely successful. Or it makes it realistic (and possible) to build a business on the side of your full-time job.

Or later, if you run a coaching business full-time, it makes it feasible to travel or take vacation without wondering where the next set of clients is going to come from, or if you're going to have to return their email to set up an appointment.

It allows you to work on your business instead of in your business.

Want to know something trippy to think about? The very same system that I created in 2014 now allows my entire team of coaches to have a continuous source of leads of people who need our help (and that we are excited to help!).

It's that same system that is making it so that I don't have to be chasing down leads and I can write this for you right now!

Is it easy to create? Simple yes, easy? No.

Worth it? Oh yes, very much so!

What you need to build an automated Client Attraction System

There are many ways to do this, but I want to show you the most simplistic form of what you need.

Let's assume that, in this case, your client attraction magnet is a PDF copy of a checklist and that you send them a video along with the checklist telling them how to use it.

NOTE: The details of the target market and the magnet are left out here because they will be very specific to your situation. What's important here as a prerequisite is that you are using something that is truly helpful and desirable that fits your target market's needs. We've almost always had to test and create several versions to get it right.

Here's what you need to make this happen:

- PDF (Client Attraction Magnet) — You can use Google Docs or Microsoft Word and Save/Export to PDF.

- Video (Made on iPhone and hosted on YouTube for free)

- Calendar Scheduling Software — We recommend ScheduleOnce or Acuity[9]

- Email Service (That allows drip email or auto-responders) — We recommend Mailchimp[10] to start.

- Landing Page — For your target market to opt-in to your Client Attraction Magnet. We recommend Leadpages,[11] or using your own hosted Wordpress site.[12]

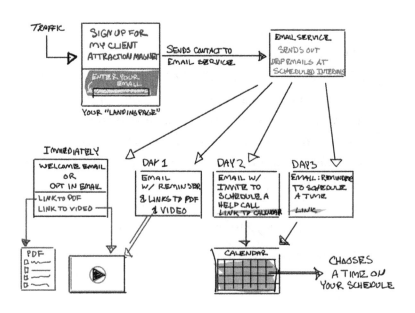

---

9 http://www.happentoyourcareer.com/acuity
10 http://happentoyourcareer.com/mailchimp
11 http://www.happentoyourcareer.com/leadpages
12 http://www.happentoyourcareer.com/how-to-create-a-wordpress-website-for-an-online-business-or-blog/

What Does a Thriving Business Look Like?

Here's what I would suggest. Start with the steps that I've outlined in this guide.

- What you don't have to spend time doing.
- Who do you actually want to work with (and can help the very most).
- How to package an offer that gets clients (because it isn't what you think).
- Creating a Client Attraction Magnet (because.... well isn't it obvious?).
- The not-so-magic trick of getting people to come to you!
- How put it on autopilot so that you can spend your time on coaching (and traveling!).

Avoid what Broke Coaches do like the plague and you will find that your coaching business rises out of the dismal abyss and your fellow coaching friends will be coming to you asking what you're doing.

Trust me, it doesn't take much. Ever since we had our first $3,000+ month many years ago, people have been beating down my door and asking to pick my brain on what we're doing.

That's how low the bar is. But you don't have to stop there. Once you know how to grow a $3,000-a-month business, you can easily do $5,000, Once you can do $5,000, simply changing your prices can get you to $8,000 a month.

$8,000 regularly per month was an important milestone for me and my family because we were used to a well above six-figure salary and didn't want to transition to full-time until we were at the cusp of that six-figure mark ($8,333 x 12 months = $100,000).

Here's the math on what a $8,000-a-month coaching business can look like.

OPTION #1: Work with 8 clients per month

If you charge $1,000/month per client and work with them for an average of 4 months, then you've reached $8,000.

$1,000 per client per month X 8 clients = $8,000

This means that you also only need to accept 2 new clients into your business each month to continue to be at 8 clients.

If you're working with just 8 clients per month, it allows you ample time to support those people and do sales and marketing and the other pieces we've mentioned in this guide. Done and Done. That's my kind of math!

Maybe that's too rich for your target market? Probably not, but I'll indulge you.

No problem.

OPTION #2: 11 Clients

If you charge $697 per month for just 11 clients this allows you get just under $8000.

12 clients a month pushes you well over the six figure mark in a given year.

This works especially well for those markets that simply don't have the excess cash to pay $1000 plus a month. It also works out if you're starting out and not yet comfortable charging higher prices.

OPTION #3: Mixed coaching, courses and speaking business

Or here's what my business looked like when I went full-time back in 2015.

Group Coaching	$ 3,500/month
One on One Coaching (3 people)	$2,700/month
Courses (created from group coaching)	$1,500
Miscellaneous (Speaking and Affiliate Income)	$1,500

Once you've built a coaching business, you don't have to keep coaching 15+ clients if you don't want to, You can mix it up any way you like.

But if you've learned all the steps earlier on in this guide, those are the same steps that you can use to develop products, courses, programs, and really to build and market businesses in your particular industry.

How Do I Make Sure That I'm Successful As a Career Coach?

I GOT TO MEET Trish when she was trying to find a program to help her understand how to build a coaching business.

She had already left her job and had a few clients.

We talked about her goals. These included creating a coaching business that provided her a full-time income. She already had a few clients, but she was used to a pretty sizeable income from her previous job as an operations executive.

We got her into our PCC program and began helping her understand a formal approach to career coaching that gave her confidence in getting her clients results, but also began focusing on growing her business.

Even though most people came into the program without already having paying clients and she was already ahead of them, Trish was struggling with where to go next.

Want to take a guess at one of the first bold moves that we helped her with?

Was it to start a massive Facebook ads campaign? No, of course not.

What about to start a podcast? Nope.

Ask all of her first clients for referrals? Sounds great and she can definitely do that, but still not it.

What was this strategic and highly impactful maneuver?

We helped her accept a job.

Wait what? Why on earth would we have her accept a job? Isn't that moving backwards? After all, she'd already achieved the dream, right? She had paying clients who were excited to work with her and was already producing income month after month.

Except that even though Trish was fortunate to have dual incomes in the family, she was still feeling financial pressure to make her business work.

The benefit of extra time that she had from not having a job and solely focusing on her business was outweighed by the stress to produce financially.

It was actually causing her to move slower!

After helping many people become coaches and build businesses, we've realized that it's a bad idea for about 90+% of the population to jump out of the plane without having ever pulled a parachute before.

Actually that analogy doesn't even remotely cover it.

Let's try again: For most human beings (even high-performers) it's a bad idea to use an airplane that isn't even fully built yet to take you up to the clouds and then solo skydive out of that same plane, when you've never tested your parachute before (or had an expert check your parachute). Add to that that you've never had a flying lesson or parachute lesson.

This is preposterous when we put it in those terms, yet that is how many of us think it's going to happen.

There are a few people we meet where it's a better situation to quit their job and jump full-time into coaching. Those people have intentionally built rather large parachutes for themselves already, and each of those chutes have several emergency ripcords in the form of cash on hand for living that meets their needs for several years if need be. These same people are those that are completely ok with those living funds being completely gone while they build a business and experience the learning along the way.

This is not the case for most people building a career coaching business. It's also not healthy for most people because, even if you have emergency funds stocked away, it still puts stressors on you that you didn't even realize could be there.

For most people who really want to set themselves up for success, it makes much more sense to plan on continuing to bring in some other "non-career coaching" income while you're building your business. Often this means building your business on the side. It also means getting help along the way.

Why?

In reality, growing a successful coaching business is a lot like learning to fly an airplane.

You could learn on your own. It's totally possible; people have done it before. But there's a high probability of crashing and burning in a way that you can't recover from.

If I'm learning to fly, I would much rather learn with someone who has done it again and successfully trained many others to fly on their own. I would want their help prepping me for what happens before I ever try a takeoff on my own.

I would want them to give me an idea of what to expect when we're up in the clouds together. I would want them to demonstrate how to fly before just handing over the controls of the plane. I would want them to be right there giving me feedback the entire time.

You're going to have failures and mistakes when you own and run any kind of business.

It will happen, but we find that the people who are successful in building and running businesses are those who set themselves up so that those mistakes and failures become learning opportunities rather than fatal mistakes.

This means that, for many people, this can be done in several ways:.

- Learn from other people who have already been there. Get help so that you're not making fatal mistakes. We offer an entire program custom-tailored specifically toward people like you who want to be professional career coaches or build a career coaching business (more about that at https://becomeacareercoach.com/certification). Even if you don't want our help, get help from people who have done this before because it will save you years of frustration or save you from becoming so frustrated that you give up.

- Take the time to set yourself up for success for the long run. We have all of our coaches create what we call a "Plan for inevitable success," identifying what they will do in advance when things go wrong (and how they will celebrate when they go right). Who will you call to support you? Who will tell you to get back on the horse? Who will take you to dinner when you get your first client?

- Create the unshakeable foundation — For some people, creating a solid foundation might mean changing jobs to something more flexible or higher paying as you're pursuing a career coaching business. For others, this might be having some very open and honest conversations with their partner that this is something that you want to pursue and that it's important to you. Communicating that you'd love their help and support as you figure out exactly what this means and what the journey looks like. Spending the time and effort to get a few things right, like a job that helps you get where you want to go or solidifying support from your family can make everything else possible.

How Do I Make Sure That I'm Successful As a Career Coach?

If you've read this far, I'm guessing you're truly interested in becoming a career coach and running a career-coaching business.

I've been there and done that and know how much the world needs this help.

If you want help, I want to support you any way that I can. To do that, I've created a whole suite of resources to help.

First and foremost, we've created a whole section of bonuses for you at https://becomeacareercoach.com/bonus including links to our tools, research, and a variety of other helpful resources to help you get your business moving.

Additionally, we've created the How to Become a Career Coach Podcast which you can search for on any podcast player including Apple iTunes, Stitcher, Overcast, and more!

This podcast shares stories from top career coaches, career coaches just starting out, and even some of the students we've worked with to help you understand what it's really like to become a career coach.

You can also find this at https://becomeacareercoach.com/podcast.

Lastly, I know how hard it is to find help on these sorts of things that is specific to your exact situation. So I want to invite you to one step further.

If you want help adapting what you've learned in this unconventional guide to your life, just email hello@happentoyourcareer.com and put "Help Becoming a Career Coach" in the subject line. My team will set aside time to help you no matter where you're at in the process. Whether you're just thinking about becoming a career coach or trying to figure out how to scale your business or someplace in between.

We will have a conversation, ask questions to understand your goals, and help get you steered in the right direction. If you want even more help beyond that, we can certainly talk about that too.

No obligation, it's our gift to you as a reader who's committed to helping others as a career coach. We do this for our readers and listeners because we know how it feels to try and start this type of business alone (difficult and not easy) and inevitably many people find out how valuable it is to have our help. We end up working with a few of those people and helping them become top career coaches in the world.

No matter what, I want you to choose at least one thing in this book to apply into the real world. Start with just one, take it forward. That's how it works. No business was built with all the sections at once.

You do one part and go on to the next. Then the next, and the next.

If you're like me and you can't stop having career and coaching type conversations with people and you want to turn this into a part time or full-time career, then there is only one way to do it.

Continuous movement. Day after day, small thing after small thing, adding up and beginning to help you get traction.

This is how it really works.

There is an entirely different life out there waiting for you. It can be fueled by a career where you get to help people create meaning in their own life and work. It's incredibly rewarding and gives you the keys to lead the type of life that you've been craving. It gives you more autonomy and flexibility than you could hope for.

In this guide, I've shown you how it's been possible for others, I've shown you examples with numbers, tried to help you understand the hard parts. I've given you permission to not do everything that you think you have to do. I've even gone to great lengths to give you examples to help you understand what this can look like for you.

At this point though, it's up to you to do something with this information. Start small and build. If you don't know where to go at any point in time, I've given you extra resources to lean on.

While you're doing all of this, I want you to keep in mind that, although this can help you live the type of life you want, at the end of the day your key to this life is by helping others without expectation or obligation.

Author, Zig Ziglar said "You can have everything in life you want, if you will just help other people get what they want."

I find this is especially true with Career Coaching.

Go forward and help others and allow that to be the ultimate influence to how you build your business.

The question everyone asks:

How do you make sure I'm successful as a career coach?

A far better (and more useful set of questions):

How do I focus on helping others? How do I take continuous small actions every day? How do I focus on a few things that help create a foundation for success to happen?

Remember the people who are most successful at building a coaching business are those who focus on helping others first. This is built into every technique and example that I've shown you along the way.

Made in the USA
Middletown, DE
14 December 2019